THE COLORADO
MOUNTAIN CLUB
PACK GUIDE

THE BEST
Colorado
Springs
HIKES

THE PIKES PEAK GROUP
of
THE COLORADO MOUNTAIN CLUB
with
GREG LONG

The Colorado Mountain Club Press
Golden, Colorado

The Best Colorado Springs Hikes
© 2009 by The Colorado Mountain Club

PUBLISHED BY

The Colorado Mountain Club Press
710 Tenth Street, Suite 200, Golden, Colorado 80401
303-996-2743   e-mail: cmcpress@cmc.org

Founded in 1912, The Colorado Mountain Club is the largest outdoor recreation, education, and conservation organization in the Rocky Mountains. Look for our books at your local bookstore or outdoor retailer or online at www.cmc.org/books.

Alan Bernhard: design, composition, and production
John Gascoyne: series editor
Greg Long: project manager
Alan Stark: publisher

CONTACTING THE PUBLISHER
We would appreciate it if readers would alert us to any errors or outdated information by contacting us at the address above.

DISTRIBUTED TO THE BOOK TRADE BY
Mountaineers Books, 1001 SW Klickitat Way, Suite 201, Seattle, WA 98134, 800-553-4453, www.mountaineerbooks.org

TOPOGRAPHIC MAPS are copyright 2009 and were created using National Geographic TOPO! Outdoor Recreation software (www.natgeomaps.com; 800-962-1643).

COVER PHOTO: Pikes Peak viewed from Rampart Range to the northeast. Photo by Todd Caudle.

We gratefully acknowledge the financial support of the people of Colorado through the Scientific and Cultural Facilities District of greater metropolitan Denver for our publishing activities.

WARNING: Although there has been an effort to make the trail descriptions in this book as accurate as possible, some discrepancies may exist between the text and the trails in the field. Hiking in mountainous areas is a high-risk activity. This guidebook is not a substitute for your experience and common sense. The users of this guidebook assume full responsibility for their own safety. Weather, terrain conditions, and individual abilities must be considered before undertaking any of the hikes in this guide.

First Edition | Second Printing

ISBN 978-0-9799663-6-1

Printed in China

DEDICATION

This book is dedicated to my father, who follows along with all of my adventures on a map, and my mother, who baked untold dozens of brownies while *not* worrying about me.

Garden of the Gods.

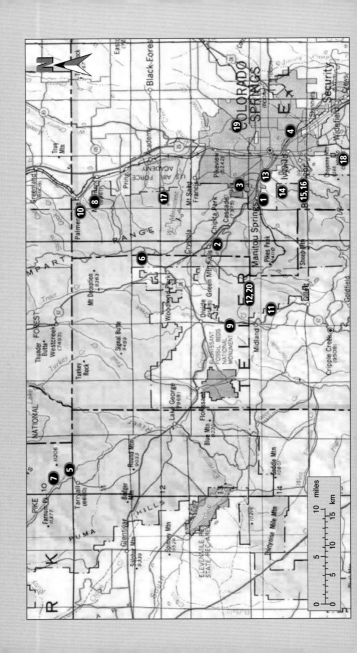

CONTENTS

ACKNOWLEDGMENTS

First and foremost, I must acknowledge Colorado Mountain Club and its members for providing friendship and companionship on countless adventures since I joined the club back in 1992. In particular, I'd like to thank Chairperson Lisa Heckel and all the members of the Pikes Peak Group who were willing to share their favorite trails and provide ideas for this guide.

Narrowing all of those great suggestions to the twenty represented here, along with many other decisions and projects along the way, was the task of the core team that made this book a reality: Bill Brown, Eric Swab, Dean Toda, and Dan Anderson of Western Maps, LLC. Dean's expertise with language and Dan's with mapping eased my workload considerably. And none of us could have done it without the leadership of series editor John Gascoyne and publisher Alan Stark.

The volunteers who gave their time to writing and photographing were invaluable to the project; it is truly their book, not mine. Some others who lent a hand and who aren't credited elsewhere are Eric Hunter, Chris Duval, Paul Doyle, Karen Ohl, Geoff Miller, and Elliott Davis.

—GREG LONG

The Pancake Rocks.   PHOTO BY BILL BROWN

Foreword

The Pikes Peak Group of The Colorado Mountain Club welcomes you to the Pikes Peak Region, gateway to Southern Colorado. The region includes Colorado Springs, Manitou Springs, Old Colorado City, Cañon City, Cripple Creek, Woodland Park, Tri-Lakes/Monument, Victor, and Green Mountain Falls. With over 300 days of sunshine annually, the region is classified as an "alpine desert" and has a moderate, dry climate. A great variety of flora and fauna can be observed while traveling along our trails.

Our members have selected a sampling of their favorite hiking trails for inclusion in this guidebook. This was not an easy undertaking as we have an abundance of hiking opportunities, literally in many of our backyards.

While the Pikes Peak Region offers numerous opportunities for our visitors, the elevations over 6,000 feet can also pose some challenges. It is easy to become dehydrated in the dry climate, so be sure to drink plenty of water. The weather can change quickly; be alert for changes and alter your plans accordingly. The Colorado Mountain Club teaches all our members to be prepared with the essential items needed to survive in case of unexpected circumstances. Always carry extra clothing and rain gear.

We take a great deal of pride in this area and ask for your help to protect the fragile environment by following Leave No Trace principles. Do not shortcut trails. Leave what you find. Pack out trash. Respect wildlife. Enjoy!

LISA HECKEL, Chairperson
Pikes Peak Group
The Colorado Mountain Club

Aspen grove along the Seven Bridges Trail to Jones Park.   PHOTO BY ERIN SHAW

Introduction

Welcome to *The Best Colorado Springs Hikes*. Let's talk about what this pack guide has to offer you.

Maybe you're a newcomer looking for a place to start exploring our great region. Maybe you're a long time resident ready to argue that a favorite hike got left out. Perhaps you're somewhere in between—just looking for new adventures and new places to explore. In any event, welcome to this collaborative effort of the Pikes Peak Group of The Colorado Mountain Club.

It was no small task to come up with the twenty best hikes in Colorado Springs. First, we defined Colorado Springs hikes as anything within an hour's drive of the city. Next, we began our deliberations with a list of over sixty possible hikes, then narrowed the list, taking several factors into consideration:

We sought diversity of geography—including areas like Palmer Lake and Monument to the north, Cripple Creek to the south, and Lost Creek Wilderness to the west. We wanted both quick jaunts right in town and remote wilderness readily accessible from town.

We looked for old standbys, like the Garden of the Gods and Barr Trail, and new areas as well—Red Rock Canyon Open Space and Cheyenne Mountain State Park have both been created within the last five years.

We included a diversity of difficulty levels: take an easy stroll along the Greenway trail or challenge your stamina hiking Barr Trail to the summit of Pikes Peak. There are hikes that can be done in an hour before or after work, a couple of all day outings, and every length in between. Most of the hikes can be done year round, while a few become excellent snowshoe outings during the winter months. Incidentally, seasoned mountaineers might attempt Pikes Peak in the winter; others should not do so.

The hikes are listed alphabetically. Browse through and see which one suits your mood and energy level on a given day.

Many of the listed hikes are mere introductions to extensive trail systems that can be explored over and over with new results every time.

If you like this sampling of hikes, consider joining the Colorado Mountain Club. The CMC sponsors numerous outings all over the state during every weekend of the year. Beyond activities like hiking and climbing, the CMC is a positive force for conservation, preservation, and education throughout the state of Colorado; it also provides a wide array of classes so members can develop their outdoors skills for the safe enjoyment of wild places like those described in this guide. See www.cmc.org for more information.

The Cheesman barn, Mueller State Park.   PHOTO BY STUART HISER

The Ten Essentials System

Hiking offers us an inexpensive and healthy way to enjoy our precious natural heritage. There can be risks that go with an outdoor adventure, however, such as encountering bad weather, suffering an injury, or getting lost. Simple advance preparation can greatly increase the likelihood of a safe and comfortable adventure. If you are not already familiar with the Ten Essential Systems, take a few minutes to study the following information and, most importantly, incorporate the Systems into all of your hiking activities.

1. **Hydration.** Water needs vary greatly, but in general carry at least two liters of water. For longer hikes, take along a water purification system. If you don't drink until you are thirsty, you have waited too long. Extra water in your vehicle will allow you to hydrate both before and after your hike.

2. **Nutrition.** Eat a good breakfast before your hike; pack a healthy lunch—fruits, vegetables, carbs, etc.—and carry some extra trail mix and/or a couple of nutrition bars in case of an emergency.

3. **Sun protection.** Include sunglasses, a large-brimmed hat, lip balm, and sunscreen with an SPF rating of 25 or higher.

4. **Insulation (extra clothing).** Colorado weather can change in an instant, at any time of year, so be prepared. Wear wool or synthetic layers of clothing. Cotton clothing retains moisture and does not insulate when it is damp—including from perspiration—so it should not be part of your hiking gear. At all times, carry a rain/wind parka and pants and extra layers of outer clothing. Gloves or mittens, a warm hat, and extra socks can be invaluable, even on a summer hike.

5. **Navigation.** Carry a map of your hiking area and a reliable—not cheap—compass. A GPS unit can add to

your ability to navigate; however, it is not a substitute for the map and compass and the ability to use them.

6. **Illumination.** Even if you plan to be back before dark, carry a headlamp or flashlight and extra batteries. A headlamp is probably the better choice—you can keep both hands free while you work or hike. (Hiking in darkness is not recommended if it can be avoided).

7. **First-aid supplies.** Include a first aid kit and know how to use it. The kit should include, at a minimum, bandages and gauze, blister protection—such as moleskin, scissors, disinfectant for cuts, toilet paper, and a ziplock bag for used t.p.

8. **Fire.** Carry waterproof matches, a lighter, fire ribbon or other commercial fire starter. Be sure that all of these will work in wet, cold, and windy conditions. Cotton dryer lint, steel wool, hardened tree sap and dry pine needles can all serve as kindling. If you are going above timberline, a small stove is a good emergency item.

9. **Repair kit and tools.** A pocketknife or multi-tool, emergency whistle, signal mirror and low-temperature electrician's tape or duct tape are handy for all types of repairs.

10. **Emergency shelter.** Carry a space blanket and parachute or other nylon cord or a bivouac sack. Large plastic leaf bags are handy for emergency rain gear, pack covers and survival shelter.

OTHER OPTIONS

Depending upon the length of the trip and the season, you may also want to include:

- A foam pad for sitting or sleeping on.
- A metal cup to melt snow in. (Trying to eat snow as a water source is not recommended).

Looking down the route, Pikes Peak from the Crags.   PHOTO BY MATT PIERCE

- A snow shovel. (A plastic disc or metal dish can be an emergency substitute).

- If you have had trouble with knees or ankles, carry a neoprene brace in your daypack—also a good cushion when eating lunch while balancing on a granite slab.

- Walking sticks—the better ones are spring-loaded and have canted handles. Walking sticks can take a great deal of weight off of your knees and legs while hiking and, at the same time, provide some upper body workout. Practice planting the tips quietly to avoid annoying your hiking companions and putting forest creatures to flight.

This information is intended as a starting place in your preparations for hiking in Colorado; it does not tell you everything that you need to know in the woods or how to deal with all emergencies. There are many programs and publications that can increase your knowledge base. Please visit The Colorado Mountain Club's website at www.cmc.org for more information.

1. Barr Trail to Pikes Peak (14,115′)

BY KEVIN BAKER

MAPS	Trails Illustrated, Pikes Peak/Cañon City, Number 137
ELEVATION GAIN	7,400 feet
RATING	Difficult
ROUND-TRIP DISTANCE	25.8 miles
ROUND-TRIP TIME	9–14 hours
NEAREST LANDMARK	Manitou Springs

COMMENT: Pikes Peak marks the end of the prairie and the beginning of Colorado's vast Rocky Mountains. It was first climbed in 1820 and has since seen millions of visitors, most by way of either the Cog Railway or the Pikes Peak Highway. Ironically, Zebulon Pike, for whom the peak is named, never made it to the summit. Katherine Lee Bates was inspired to write "America the Beautiful" atop the mountain, earning Pikes the nickname "America's Mountain." Although not at all technically challenging, a trek up Barr Trail to the summit of Pikes is a worthy accomplishment.

Pikes via Barr Trail has the most vertical gain of any 14er in Colorado. A dayhike of Pikes is a huge day, so most folks split up the hike into at least two days, with a stay at Barr Camp, some 6.5 miles up the trail, at 10,200 feet. Barr Camp offers many accommodations including a main bunkhouse, a private cabin, lean-to shelters, and tent sites. Breakfast and dinner are available by reservation, and hot and cold drinks are sold all day. This historic place sees over 20,000 visitors per year, with most coming in the summer. Visit www.barrcamp.com for information on rates or to make reservations.

GETTING THERE: From U.S. 24, take the Manitou Springs exit and turn west onto Manitou Avenue. Continue 1.4 miles west to

The trail near Lightning Point.

Ruxton Avenue. Turn left on Ruxton and continue up this narrow road 1.0 mile to Hydro Street, just beyond the parking area for the cog railway. Go right on Hydro and up the steep, narrow street to the trailhead. Parking may be difficult. On weekends, you may have to park below the cog railway on Ruxton.

THE ROUTE: Barr Trail has a variety of terrain that will challenge every peakbagger. The first 3.0 miles of trail will test you with a series of switchbacks up the steep southeast slopes. After passing under a natural rock arch, the trail zigs its way steeply up the south slopes, then gradually heads west, contouring along the south slopes of Rocky Mountain. Continue west at the trail junction with a spur trail that leads to the top of the incline.

After 3.2 miles, a sign at No Name Creek advises Barr Camp is only 3.5 miles away. Most of the vertical to Barr Camp is done and the rest of the way is much easier. Be aware that every trail sign indicating mileage will be utterly wrong. Head left at the sign, following the creek for a bit. Be sure to stay right at the junction with the unsigned Pipeline Trail. Miss and you can end up in Ruxton Park!

After a few more steep switchbacks, the terrain mellows out and there are flat sections to recuperate on. Some of the best views of Pikes can be obtained by scrambling just off the trail. Lightning Point is a rock outcropping just a few yards off the trail to the south, beyond the *7.8 miles to summit* sign. Monte's View Rockpile is a fun scramble just 1.0 mile from Barr Camp south of the trail, although you'll have to do some rough bushwhacking to get up it!

The section from No Name Creek offers some nice downhill options for a change of pace. After a few steeper sections, you finally arrive at Barr Camp. Barr is a good place to refuel and fill up your water if you're dayhiking, although the water is untreated and requires purification. Barr Camp has Gatorade, bottled water, and snacks.

The second half of the hike to the summit is much tougher, due to the thinning air, but the many switchbacks keep the

Approaching Barr Camp.

Hiking into the clouds.

overall steepness of the trail manageable. I like to break
this journey into segments: the first is Barr Camp to the
Bottomless Pit Trail. A series of long switchbacks leads up
the forest, with beautiful bristlecone pine trees along the way.
The trail is quite a bit rockier above Barr Camp, but wide and
easy to follow. After 1.0 mile, there is a sign for the Bottomless
Pit, an enchanting place below the north face of Pikes that
few people get a chance to visit. Bottomless Pit is at the base
of the Y and Railroad couloirs, a couple of fun, moderate
snow climbs for experienced mountaineers using technical
climbing gear. Be sure to take the switchback left at this trail
junction.

The trail then zigs and zags its way up to A-Frame, a shelter
that some opt to camp at, near treeline at 12,000 feet. I find
this section of the hike to be the longest. In winter, with
decent snow conditions, a viable option from treeline is to
follow a prominent low-angle gully of snow all the way up to
the summit. Other times, follow short switchbacks to around
12,800 feet, at the base of where the east ridge steepens. The

trail then does a long traverse across the broad east face, gently climbing 400 feet to a view down into a dramatic bowl known as the Cirque. Enjoy what is probably the most dramatic spot along the trail.

After a few short switchbacks along the edge of the Cirque, there is a sign announcing one mile to the summit. The trail zigs its way up the upper east face, with a few shorter traverses, until the infamous *16 Golden Stairs*, a reference to the number of switchbacks left on the trail—there are actually 32 of them. The trail now gets rockier and requires clambering over boulders, but keep pressing on and you'll soon pop out at the end of the train tracks. The summit is not your typical 14er, as you will likely be sharing it with tourists who have either ridden the cog railway or driven up the Pikes Peak Highway.

It is sometimes possible to either ride the train or hitch a ride down, but don't count on it happening. Be prepared to make the long slog all the way back to the bottom. Make certain to visit the true summit of Pikes, amid an indistinct jumble of boulders in the middle of the parking lot. Donuts and pizza are available at the summit house, a rare treat on a 14er. Barr Trail is a classic that anyone in decent shape can experience—give it a shot.

See if you can still count at this altitude.   PHOTO BY PAUL DOYLE

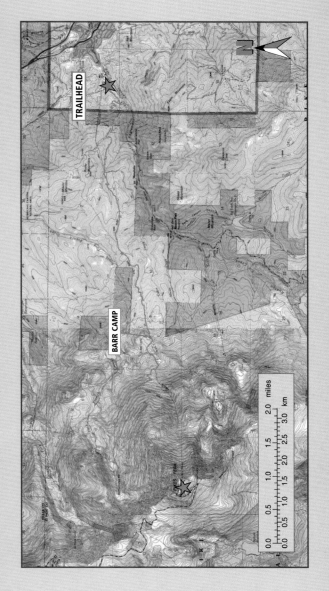

TRAILHEAD

BARR CAMP

| 0.0 | 0.5 | 1.0 | 1.5 | 2.0 miles |
| 0.0 | 0.5 | 1.0 | 1.5 | 2.0 | 2.5 | 3.0 km |

2. Catamount Trail

BY DR. TRAJN BOUGHAN

MAPS	Trails Illustrated, Pikes Peak/Cañon City, Number 137
ELEVATION GAIN	1,400 feet
RATING	Easy–moderate
ROUND-TRIP DISTANCE	5.5 miles
ROUND-TRIP TIME	2–4 hours
NEAREST LANDMARK	Green Mountain Falls

COMMENT: The town of Green Mountain Falls hosts a city park on a mountain slope—the Catamount Trail. The trail scales a sidewall of the Ute Pass, a slot canyon rising from Manitou Springs into the Rocky Mountains. Catamount Creek, and nearby Crystal Creek, fall from the canyon's edge. Catamount is another name for a Colorado mountain lion.

The Catamount Trail is an out-and-back trip between Green Mountain Falls and the North and South Catamount and Crystal Creek Reservoirs. Start early enough to return before summer thunderstorms. The trail is well maintained and easy to follow, with little blue-dots nailed to the trees.

GETTING THERE: Take U.S. 24 west from Colorado Springs. From the traffic light at Cascade, drive about 4 miles and take the second exit marked Green Mountain Falls, Chipita Park. The ramp drops into the commercial district; park on the main street, Ute Pass Avenue.

THE ROUTE: The hike's staging area is downtown, with two ways to reach the wilderness trailhead. The northern approach, by Belvedere Avenue, ascends gradually. The more direct, more demanding, southerly route climbs straight up to the top of Hondo Avenue. The Catamount Trail officially begins at the waterworks' road bridge on Hondo Avenue.

A trailside cascade.   PHOTO BY DR. TRAJN BOUGHAN

The zigzag route gains elevation quickly and keeps returning to the creek side, allowing water play at tiny beaches. Many hikers are content to reach the waterfall, where the color-coded trail markers diverge. An informal tied-log footbridge, topped by teetering flat stones, allows a stream crossing to join the yellow-dot Thomas Trail. This connects back to the upper reaches of Boulder Street in town.

The Catamount's diversionary trail veers away from the creek and takes a long northerly traverse, headed toward a saddle in the ridge above. A narrow single-track skirts the base of the Dome Rock outcropping. An optional short spur steps up to a rocky promontory overlooking the town. Look across the valley to see how far the opposite Rampart Range ridgeline keeps dropping while your own climb gains altitude.

Near the crest, a forest of blue-dots guides you across sheer rock whose thin soils cannot hold a constructed trail bed. The hard climb is finally over once you've reached the cross path. Long-distance views open down both sides of the knife-edge ridge. Turquoise-dot signs point out another spur for a panoramic view over Ute Pass.

The main trail of the plain blue-dots drops from the ridge, going straight down into a fanciful place called The Garden of Eden. The packed-dirt path moves into a sunny meadow. The south slope, covered in spruce, fir, and ponderosa pine, is confronted across the valley floor by a high, wavy wall of granular granite, wind-whipped to form hoodoo columns. Catamount Creek reappears as an innocent meander through a marsh, with broad-leaf vegetation, shadowed groves, juvenile blue spruce succeeding aspens after a fire, and seasonal wildflowers.

Ambitious hikers can walk further, after crossing the low creek on a log, to find the South Catamount Reservoir. Engineered scenery disrupts the natural ambience beyond the gate, where a dusty service road passes underneath the reservoir's massive rubble wall. Red raspberries ripen by the roadside in the end of August, sweetening the outlook. A view of Pikes Peak greets your arrival at the top of the dam. Families drive in from the Pikes Peak Toll Road to picnic and motorboat. Look down to see anglers settled in chairs portaged from the parking lot. Be sure to return to the gate by 4 PM, when the reservoir park closes for the day.

Living the good life.   PHOTO BY DR. TRAJN BOUGHAN

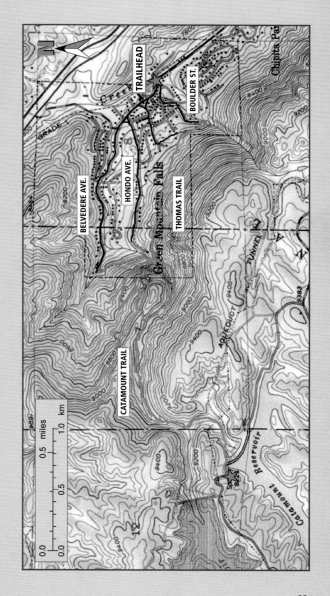

3. Garden of the Gods

BY BILL HOUGHTON

MAPS	Trails Illustrated, Pikes Peak/Cañon City Number 137 USGS, Colorado Springs, 7.5 minute Visitor Center Trail Map
ELEVATION GAIN	200 feet
RATING	Easy
LOOP DISTANCE	3 miles
LOOP TIME	1.5 hours
NEAREST LANDMARK	This is IT

COMMENT: The Garden of the Gods, a 1,320-acre Colorado Springs city park, is the place to go for great viewing and enjoyment of nature at her best. The park is popular in all seasons. Its numerous trails lend themselves to exploration and provide a variety of perspectives on the magnificent rock formations—the remains of an ancient beach tipped 90 degrees. Paved interior trails in the Central Garden are handicapped-accessible. Abundant wildlife enjoy the Garden.

GETTING THERE: From downtown, take U.S. 24 west 3.1 miles to the 31st Street exit. Turn right, go to the first signal and turn right again, on Colorado Avenue. Go one block, turn left on 30th Street and go 2.0 miles, through two traffic lights. The primary access to the park is via Gateway Road, across the street from the Garden of the Gods Visitor Center. Once on Gateway Road, go 0.4 mile west to a "T" intersection, then right (north) on the one-way Juniper Way for 0.3 mile. Around the curve are the main (north) parking lot and the primary access to the trails.

THE ROUTE: Following at least five named trails—Bretag, Ute, Buckskin Charley, Scotsman, and Palmer—you can make a loop outside the paved road around the Central Garden.

A dusting of snow in Garden of the Gods.

PHOTO BY DANIELLE LAROSE

Start the loop from the north parking lot by walking north and crossing Juniper Way. At a trail "T" intersection, turn right and start a clockwise loop. This first segment, Susan Bretag Trail, takes you through open fields with great views of the North Gateway Rock and the park's signature rock feature, the Kissing Camels.

The Bretag Trail ends at 0.5 mile, at the east access, Gateway Road. Cross the road and take the right fork to pick up the Ute Trail. The trail skirts the west edge of an old city reservoir and climbs to the south garden parking lot. Cross the parking lot to continue the Ute Trail on the south side of the lot. As it starts up the hill toward the parking lot, the Ute Trail splits; take the trail to the right. At 1.2 miles, take an unmarked smaller trail to the right, to a crossing of the south park access road (Ridge Road).

To continue the loop, cross Ridge Road and you are on the Buckskin Charlie Trail. Go up and over a short hill and take the first right turn. Follow this trail north to an intersection, at 1.75 miles, with the Scotsman Trail, the primary horse trail used by stable riders. A right turn onto the trail, at 2.0 miles, leads to a short spur trail to the Central Garden. Take the spur trail to Juniper Way. Walk left (north) up the road, past the intersection where Garden Drive splits off toward Balanced Rock, and other sights, in the southwest corner of the park, to a left turnoff about 30 yards up the road from the intersection. A short access leads to a trail intersection, where the Palmer Trail goes in both directions, with the Siamese Twins to the south. Go north to complete the loop.

This part of the Palmer Trail leads to picturesque views of the Central Garden and all the rocks to the east. This is particularly inspiring in the early morning and at sunset. The trail climbs steeply to several good overlooks before going down and around the north end of North Gateway Rock. Here, the trail connects to the start and the north parking lot, at 3.0 miles.

SIDEBAR: MORE ROUTES

To add some distance and another famous rock formation, an extension on the Scotsman Trail leads to the Siamese Twins. Measuring from the intersection of the Scotsman Trail with the spur to the Central Garden, as described above, remain on the Scotsman Trail for another 0.5 mile. Descend past low-lying sandstone formations, pass the Scotsman Picnic Area on the right, and continue to a sign that reads *To Palmer Trail*. Cross the paved road to the west. Join the Palmer Trail and go left, or south. To return, reverse your track on the Palmer Trail but stay on it as it parallels the road north, rejoining the trail described above, at 0.8 mile.

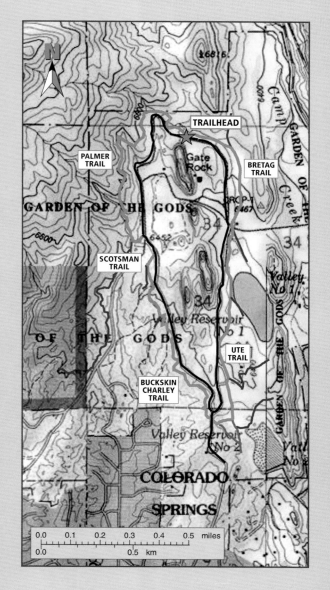

4. Greenway Trail

BY DEAN TODA

MAPS	USGS, Colorado Springs/Pikeview, 7.5 minute
ELEVATION GAIN	550 feet
RATING	Easy
ROUND-TRIP DISTANCE	From 1–28.4 miles
ROUND-TRIP TIME	Spend an hour or a day

COMMENT: Pristine it ain't, but convenience makes the Pikes Peak Greenway the most popular trail in Colorado Springs. Spend an hour or a day on this downtown gem. Following Fountain and Monument Creeks, the Greenway is the aorta of the city's 105-mile urban trail system. It's also a part of the Front Range Trail, which, as of 2008, was continuous from Fountain to the Greenland Open Space. Much of the Greenway is well-graded dirt and gravel, but there are long stretches of asphalt and even some concrete. Its 12-foot width and gentle inclines accommodate all manner of non-motorized users: walkers, runners, horseback riders, Nordic skiers after a good snowfall and, especially, cyclists.

GETTING THERE: Most Colorado Springs residents live within walking distance of the Greenway or one of its 15 feeder trails. To drive, the better trailhead parking lots are at El Pomar Youth Sports Complex, south of Circle Drive; at the end of Cache La Poudre Street, in Monument Valley Park; the Gossage Youth Sports Complex, off Mark Dabling Boulevard north of Fillmore Street; and on the north side of Woodmen Road, just west of Interstate 25.

THE ROUTE: The Greenway starts on the eastern edge of El Pomar Youth Sports Center—Mile 25, according to the milepost, one of a series planted every 0.5 mile along the

Not hills, but walls to climb along the Greenway Trail.   PHOTO BY GREG LONG

route. From this point, it's 7.0 miles south on the Front Range Trail to Fountain Creek Regional Park. But you're heading north, so Fountain Creek, lined with the cottonwoods and dense bottomland underbrush that characterize most of the trail, is on your right.

The trail passes under Circle Drive at 0.7 mile and, at 1.5 miles (Milepost 26.5), it crosses to the northeast bank of the creek on the first of many wood-decked trestle bridges. Recross the creek at 2.4 miles on another wooden bridge. For the next 0.5 mile you're a stone's throw from I-25.

At 3.0 miles (Milepost 28), recross the creek on a concrete low-water bridge. Use caution following periods of rain: Fountain Creek can become a powerful torrent after a storm.

Follow the creek west under Nevada Avenue and Tejon Street and, at 3.4 miles, come to the Greenway's biggest natural jewel: the Tejon Marsh—an improbable oasis of cattails and wading birds with I-25 and the Motor City car-dealer complex as a backdrop.

After the next bridge crossing, at 4.2 miles, go right (left is the trail to Bear Creek Regional County Park). At 4.5 miles (Milepost 29.5), the trail dips under Cimarron Street, then over Fountain Creek a few yards above its confluence with Monument Creek. From here, the trail leaves Fountain Creek and follows Monument Creek northward.

Stay straight at 4.7 miles. Left is the Midland Trail, heading northwest to Old Colorado City, and right is a bridge to America the Beautiful Park. At 5.2 miles, cross a low-water bridge, pass under Bijou Street, bear right up a ramp and enter Monument Valley Park. Here you'll find the heaviest foot and bicycle traffic, as well as your first encounter with motor vehicles—a grade crossing of Cache La Poudre Street, at 5.9 miles.

Continuing north past the campus of Colorado College, the trail follows the broad back of a levee. Shortly after leaving Monument Valley Park, at 7.4 miles, follow signs

Jogging through, near downtown Colorado Springs.   PHOTO BY GREG LONG

An underpass near Uintah Street.

for a 200-yard detour around a disused railroad spur that puts you on Beacon Street for a few strides.

Rejoining Monument Creek, cross to the west bank on a concrete trestle bridge, at 7.9 miles and, at 8.1 miles, come to the Greenway's last grade crossing, at Polk Street.

Meandering northward past the Gossage Youth Sports Complex, at 9.7 miles, you'll pass a bridge leading to the Templeton Gap Trail, which links to Palmer Park.

The Pikeview Reservoir comes into view at 10.1 miles, after which the trail dives under Garden of the Gods Road. Recross the creek, at 10.7 miles and 11.2 miles. At 11.8 miles, pass under I-25; the rest of the trail is west of the interstate.

After another bridge, at 12.0 miles (milepost 37), the trail makes a sharp left, at 12.8 miles, onto a bridge spanning Cottonwood Creek. At the end of the bridge go left again to rejoin Monument Creek.

A ribbon of stone graces the Greenway Trail.

At 13.2 miles, bear left onto gravel and recross to the west side of the creek to pass under Woodmen Road. By 13.5 miles (Milepost 38.5), the trail leaves Monument Creek and begins to parallel the Union Pacific railroad tracks, heading northwest. Cottonwoods give way to pines and road noise recedes as the trail enters its most pastoral section. The interlude is brief because, at 14.2 miles, you reach a sign marking the end of the Greenway and the beginning of the New Santa Fe Trail. This is the Front Range Trail's next leg, which traverses the Air Force Academy to Monument and beyond.

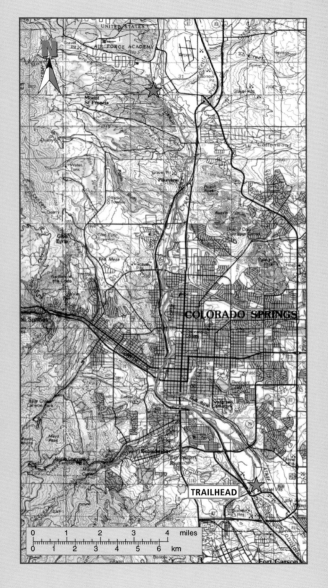

TRAILHEAD

COLORADO SPRINGS

| 0 | 1 | 2 | 3 | 4 | miles |

| 0 | 1 | 2 | 3 | 4 | 5 | 6 | km |

5. Lizard Rock – Lake Park Loop

BY GREG LONG

MAPS	Trails Illustrated, Tarryall Mountains/ Kenosha Pass, Number 105
ELEVATION GAIN	Lizard Rock: 1,000 feet; full loop: 3,600 feet
RATING	Lizard Rock: easy–moderate; full loop: moderate–difficult
ROUND-TRIP DISTANCE	Lizard Rock: 5 miles; full loop: 15.1 miles
ROUND-TRIP TIME	Lizard Rock: 2–3 hours; full loop: 7–10 hours
NEAREST LANDMARK	Lake George

COMMENT: Most of this loop lies within the Lost Creek Wilderness, a pristine area found—incredibly—within an hour's drive of both Colorado Springs and Denver. Be it summer wildflowers, fall's colors, unique granite formations, or just a quiet space for meditation and reflection, Lost Creek provides it.

The Lizard Rock Trail provides a short outing over mild terrain to its namesake rock formation and great views of the wilderness and, all the way west, the Sawatch Range. Continuing the loop over Hankins Pass to Lake Park provides an intense all-day workout or delightful weekend backpack. The trail is well maintained with good signage throughout.

The Lost Creek Wilderness has many interconnecting trails, allowing for excellent multi-day backpacking opportunities, of which this loop is just one.

GETTING THERE: Take U.S. 24 west from Colorado Springs for 37 miles to Lake George and turn right onto County Road 77. Travel 12.8 miles and turn right, into Spruce Grove Campground. Dayhikers should park outside the fence; the trail leaves from inside the campground, behind the pit toilets.

Lake Park. PHOTO BY GREG LONG

THE ROUTE: Cross the bridge over the creek and take an immediate left onto Lizard Rock Trail #658. Pass through a short rock tunnel and stay on the main track, over gentle ups and downs and through open meadows with views of the rock formations above. Switchbacks and a steeper grade begin after 2.0 miles; at 2.3. miles, take the right fork for the loop towards Lake Park, or take a hard left for the side trail to Lizard Rock. To get to the Rock, scramble steeply for 0.25 mile and enjoy great 360-degree views of the Lost Creek Wilderness.

To continue on the loop, pass the *Wilderness* sign and, at 2.4 miles, take another right fork. Trail #658 becomes Trail #630. Look for a sign indicating, *To Lake Park/Goose Creek Campground* (the sign is not visible until after the turn) and follow up well-graded switchbacks to Hankins Pass, at 3.9 miles. At the pass, turn left (west) on Lake Park Trail #639. The trail climbs steeply along a ridge towards Lake Park. Pause to scramble up one of the many rock formations and take in the views. Look back to the southeast to see the burn scar from the 2002 Hayman Fire, which started in this area

Fall colors near Hankins Pass.

and burned over 138,000 acres. At 5.7 miles, descend into Lake Park, an open area with wildflowers, rock formations and excellent fall colors. Level camping spots are plentiful and water is available at the west end of the park.

After many ups and downs, the trail finally tops out at 7.4 miles, at 11,580 feet. Begin descending on steep, loose trail before the angle lessens in a lush coniferous forest. At 8.6 miles, watch for a sign indicating the *Brookside Trail #607*. Turn left (south) and follow the Brookside Trail for two miles, where it connects back with Trail #658. There are additional good camping spots along here. Turn left (southeast) at the *Spruce Grove C.G.3, Hankins Pass 3* sign and climb back to the saddle with the Lizard Rock turnoff. Follow Trail #658 back to the parking area.

SIDEBAR: **McCURDY MOUNTAIN**

The Lake Park loop can be connected with the McCurdy Mountain Trail, Hike No. 7 in this guide. At 8.6 miles in the directions above, turn north instead of south on Trail #607 to reach McCurdy Mountain. This could make a scenic additional day on a backpack trip or a challenging side trip for a dayhiking masochist.

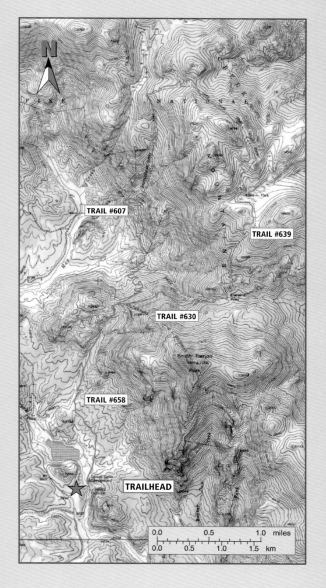

TRAIL #607

TRAIL #639

TRAIL #630

TRAIL #658

TRAILHEAD

| 0.0 | 0.5 | 1.0 miles |
| 0.0 | 0.5 | 1.0 | 1.5 km |

6. Lovell Gulch

BY ALEX PAUL

MAPS	Trails Illustrated, Pikes Peak/Cañon City, Number 137
ELEVATION GAIN	1,000 feet
RATING	Easy–moderate
ROUND-TRIP DISTANCE	5.5 miles
ROUND-TRIP TIME	3 hours
NEAREST LANDMARK	Woodland Park

COMMENT: Lovell Gulch is a pleasant loop trail winding through the sub-alpine ponderosa/spruce forest of the Rocky Mountain foothills. The gulch offers views of open ponderosa pine and grassy meadows on south facing slopes and thick spruce forest covering the north facing slopes. The meadows and forest display a wide variety of wildflowers throughout the growing season, from wild iris and lady slippers in early summer to thistle and mariposa lily later in summer, and a myriad of flowers that bloom throughout the summer. The secluded valleys are habitat for mule deer, elk, bear, fox, and coyote. Wildlife is commonly observed from the trail early in the morning or near dusk.

Outlooks from the high point of the loop trail afford panoramic views of Wilkerson Pass, Crystal Peak, the Tarryall Mountains, the Hayman Fire burn area and, on clear days, the snow capped peaks of the Sawatch Range far to the west. Descending the ridge on the backside of the loop allows glimpses of Pikes Peak through the trees to the south.

Lovell Gulch is also a popular trail with equestrians and mountain bikers. Dogs are allowed, but keep them under control in order not to disturb wildlife and other trail users.

GETTING THERE: From the U.S. 24/Cimarron exit, Number 141, on Interstate 25, take U.S. 24 west 17.2 miles to Woodland Park.

Pikes Peak North Face.

At the third stop light in Woodland Park, in view of the City of Woodland Park sign, turn right onto Baldwin Street. Proceed 2.1 miles, passing the high school campus, where Baldwin Street becomes Rampart Range Road, to the City of Woodland Park maintenance shop on the left. Pull off and park along the fence south of the shop. The trailhead is visible to the west. Proceed through the gate in the fence to access the trail.

THE ROUTE: The Lovell Gulch Trail is generally well defined and consists of a wide single-track or narrower double-track paths. It is well graded with fine granite gravel covering the tread, with only scattered washouts.

From the gate, follow the trail for about 0.5 mile along the edge of the city shop and some residences. Continue on through the forest to a trail intersection at 0.8 mile. Take the left fork down and across the creek. (Save the right fork for some future variation.) Across the creek a sign marks the start of the Lovell Gulch Loop Trail (3¾ miles). Take the right fork and hike the trail counter-clockwise. The trail follows the

Time out for some bouldering opportunities.

creek along the bottom of Lovell Gulch, with ponderosa pine on the left slope and heavy spruce on the right. As the trail ascends the gulch, the valley narrows, with large granite boulders on the slopes close to the trail.

At 2.4 miles, the trail tops at Rampart Range Road. Walk left through the vehicle barricade and follow under the power line to the west. At 3.3 miles, the trail crosses under the power line and veers northwest away from it. The trail then climbs a knoll, with grand views of Pikes Peak, Woodland Park and the mountains to the west. From this knoll, the trail drops steeply to the west until it turns south and follows along the boundary fence between National Forest and privately owned land, back to the *Lovell Gulch Loop* sign. Bear right and follow the previously taken access trail back to the parking lot.

LOVELL GULCH LOOP TRAIL

TRAILHEAD

7. McCurdy Mountain

BY ERIC SWAB

MAPS	Trails Illustrated, Tarryall Mountains/ Kenosha Pass, Number 105 USGS, McCurdy Mountain, 7.5 minute
ELEVATION GAIN	4,270 feet
RATING	Difficult
ROUND-TRIP DISTANCE	17.25 miles
ROUND-TRIP TIME	8–10 hours
NEAREST LANDMARK	Twin Eagles Campground on County Rd. 77

COMMENT: McCurdy Mountain's 12,168-foot summit is the second highest in the Tarryall Mountains, part of the Lost Creek Wilderness. Lost Creek is renowned for its incredible red granite rock formations. Unlike many of the Rocky Mountains' broken crags, these are soft and convoluted, forming fanciful shapes.

The destination campground is a Pike National Forest fee area, and parking for the day is $3.00, or $1.50 with a Golden Age Passport. Registration for entry into the Wilderness is free. It helps the Forest Service track use of the area and provides the hiker with information about its protection.

There is a pit toilet south of the main parking area. Dogs on a leash and horses are permitted on the trail. Bicycles are not allowed in the Wilderness.

In summer carry three to four liters of water, less if you have a filter or tablets. A compass will help with off-trail route finding near the summit, especially if clouds move in and obscure the landmarks.

GETTING THERE: From Colorado Springs take U.S. 24 west; 1.0 mile west of the town of Lake George, turn right at the sign to Tarryall. Follow Park County Road 77 for 17 miles to the Twin Eagles Campground, at 8,550 feet.

Enjoying the rock formations.

THE ROUTE: The trailhead is at the north end of the campground parking lot. From the trailhead, cross a bridge over Tarryall Creek and turn left. The wilderness registration box is at 0.4 mile. Turn left onto the old wagon road, Forest Service Trail 607. A sign at 2.1 miles says *Twin Eagles TH 2*, pointing back the way you came, and *McCurdy Park 4*, pointing in the direction you want. The side trail sign says *Spruce Grove C.G. 3, Hankins Pass 3*.

Climbing gets serious at 2.75 miles. At 3.0 miles, watch for Lizard Rock, a large formation perched on top of a treed knob, across the valley to the southwest. At 3.25 miles, enter the Lost Creek Wilderness Area. Watch for a rock window on your left, with a rock needle sticking up in the middle, around 4.25 miles. At 5.2 miles, reach a saddle and another junction signed, *Lake Park Tr No. 639*, to the right and *Brookside Trail No. 607*, your route, straight ahead. The trail descends here to a stream crossing and your last chance to refill your water containers.

As you climb out of this drainage, you will come to another junction. The sign announces *McCurdy Park Tr.*

Granite spires.   PHOTO BY ERIC SWAB

No. 628, straight ahead, and *Brookside Tr. No. 607*, to the left.
Stay on 607. At 6.8 miles, enter the realm of the silver-gray
ghosts of a forest fire that predated 1898. These weathered
snags, set against the backdrop of red granite ramparts,
compose some of the finest natural sculpture in Colorado.

At 7.0 miles you will begin to see young limber and
bristlecone pine growing, probably the descendants of the
burned trees. From here, cross three minor ridges. At the
third ridge, mile 8, you will leave the trail. There is no sign.
Please do not follow in someone else's footsteps—this will
lessen your impact on the fragile alpine tundra.

Begin your off-trail excursion on compass heading 30°,
toward the lowest point on the horizon. Passing above the
long, low ridge of layered granite, you will be in a broad valley
between two rocky ridges. Stay low in the valley until you are
near the saddle. This will allow you to judge which rock outcropping is the highest. The outcroppings to the right and left
are both McCurdy. The one to the southeast (right) is 4 feet
higher and is the actual summit. The easiest scramble to the
top is from the northeast, to the climber's left. There are just a
few moves for which you will need to use your hands.

From the summit you have a 360° view of the world. At
10° is Windy Peak (11,970 feet) and at 50° is Buffalo Peak
(11,589 feet), both in the Lost Creek Wilderness. At 100° is
the 2002 Hayman Fire area; at 115° is Pikes Peak (14,115
feet); at 250° is the Sawatch Range and at 330°, Bison Peak
(12,431 feet). Return the way you came.

TRAILHEAD

8. Mount Herman

BY KATE STEWART

MAPS	Trails Illustrated, Pikes Peak/Cañon City, Number 137
ELEVATION GAIN	1,000 feet
RATING	Easy–moderate
ROUND-TRIP DISTANCE	2.1 miles
ROUND-TRIP TIME	1–2 hours
NEAREST LANDMARK	Town of Monument/Pikes Peak Hot Shots Fire Center.

COMMENT: Forest Service Trail # 716 offers a quiet, usually secluded hike. The path is steep, rough, and eroded. It can be treacherous on a rainy day. Mount Herman has been climbed for years. A CMC hike was reported on this trail in 1913. It is still beautiful and wild.

GETTING THERE: From Colorado Springs, take Interstate 25 North to the Monument exit (exit 161). Turn left at the light at the end of the exit ramp onto Highway 105. Follow this road back across I-25 and go straight through the lights, onto Second Street.

Follow Second Street across a set of railroad tracks to a stop sign at Mitchell Avenue. (It is approximately 1.0 mile from the exit ramp to this stop sign.) Turn left and follow Mitchell Avenue for 0.6 mile. Turn right onto Mt. Herman Road. In 1.5 miles, this road turns from pavement to dirt. The trailhead is 3.3 miles from where the pavement ends and the dirt begins.

Note that there is a Mount Herman trailhead at the corner of Nursery Road and Mount Herman Road. Don't get confused: your trailhead is several miles farther. Mount Herman road is a four-wheel-drive road. It is rutted and challenging, but manageable in passenger cars. Use extra caution if the weather is rainy.

Air Force Academy Chapel in the distance.

The trailhead is at a tight left turn in the road. It will be on the right and has space for about seven cars. There are no signs at the trailhead, so rely on your odometer.

A trail marker, Forest Service Trail # 716, is on the right of the trail as you begin your hike.

THE ROUTE: The well used trail follows a small mountain stream on your left. Watch for false trails that lead off from the main trail.

You will pass through a flower-filled meadow. We identified purple asters, black-eyed Susans, purple bee balm, large blue bells, and tiny blue harebells. This hike is not very long, but it makes up for the distance by the aggressive uphill climb of 1,000 feet in just over a mile.

The path follows the stream until it turns to the right and goes up a hill. At this fork, a faint, dead-end trail leads off to the left.

Instead, follow the trail to the right and up the hill until it switchbacks to the left and leads upwards through the trees.

Looking towards Cap Rock from the summit.

The trail is eroded and water run off is apparent. At this turn, there is another trail leading off to the right to a nice overlook.

After 0.75 mile, the trail turns to the right and continues steeply through rockfall. Cairns lead the way through the rocks. Once up the rockfall, a meadow leads to a steep drop-off to the valley below. There is a long summit ridge; the highpoint is at the furthest left (north) side of the ridge. From here, there are lovely views of Monument and its surrounding lakes, the Air Force Academy, and Pikes Peak to the south. On a clear day, you may see Mt. Evans and Longs Peak to the north.

Spend some time at the top. There is plenty of shade and there are plenty of photo opportunities. It is a great place for a picnic if you want.

You return on the same trail, and now the words are: steep downhill, watch your footing. Regardless of the ups and the downs of the trail, the views make it all worthwhile. Enjoy.

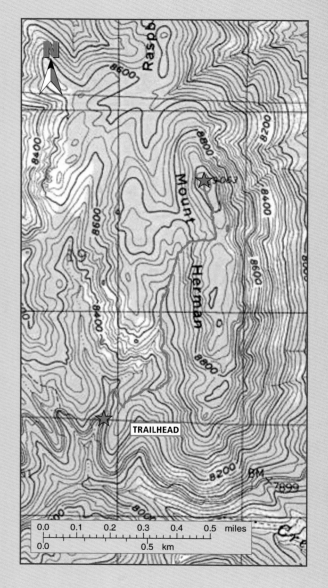

N

8600

Raspb

8200

8400

8800

8053

8400

8600

8600

8800

8400

8800

TRAILHEAD

8200

BM
7899

8000

| 0.0 | 0.1 | 0.2 | 0.3 | 0.4 | 0.5 | miles |

| 0.0 | | | 0.5 | | | km |

9. Mueller State Park – Cheesman Ranch and Outlook Ridge Geer Pond Loop

BY STUART HISER

MAPS	Trails Illustrated, Pikes Peak/Cañon City, Number 137 Visitor's Center trail map
ELEVATION GAIN	Cheesman: 1,200 feet; Outlook: 800 feet
RATING	Cheesman: moderate; Outlook: easy
ROUND-TRIP DISTANCE	Cheesman: 8–8.5 miles; Outlook: 4–4.5 miles
ROUND-TRIP TIME	Cheesman: 4–5 hours; Outlook: 1.5–2 hours
NEAREST LANDMARK	Divide, CO

COMMENT: Mueller State Park provides over 50 miles of varied hiking trails within 45 minutes of town. The Cheesman Ranch hike includes the Cheesman Ranch homestead. Although closed, most buildings are largely intact. There are views of the west side of Pikes Peak, and herds of elk are not uncommon. In the fall, the aspen groves are in full color. The ranch offers many shady spots for a picnic lunch, while the easy Outlook Ridge Geer Pond Loop hike introduces you to the trails at Mueller. This part of the park is closed in late spring for elk calving.

There is a park entrance fee per vehicle per visit.

GETTING THERE: From Colorado Springs, take U.S. 24 west to Divide. Turn left (south) on Colorado 67 and continue 5.0 miles to the park entrance. Follow the main road through the park, into the campground, to the Peak View trailhead. There is water and a restroom at this trailhead.

Peak View Pond.

THE ROUTE:

CHEESMAN RANCH: Begin east on Trail #19, Peak View. Pass Peak View Pond on your right (a spur trail leads down to the pond). At the junction with Trail #18, Elk Meadow, turn left (north). Where this trail joins with Trail #17, Cheesman Ranch, continue straight ahead (north). The trail passes Rule Creek Pond as it makes it way northward through an open meadow. At the far north end of the park, the trail bears west as it passes the Cheesman Ranch homestead. Past the homestead, the trail turns back to the south and starts a long climb uphill into the trees. To your right, you will pass Trail #32, Dynamite Cabin—an optional 1.0 mile side loop that rejoins Trail #17.

Not far from the campground, the trail comes to a three-way junction. Here you could take Trail #16 to the top of Grouse Mountain overlook, about a 0.5 mile out-and-back, for some nice views and a good place to stop for lunch.

Sentinel Point.

From the three-way junction, trail #17 continues east. At the junction with trail #35 (Lost Still), there is another optional side loop to Cahil Pond: turn left on trail #35, right on trail #34 (Cahil Pond), right on trail #36 (Moonshine), and finally rejoin trail #17 to your left. Where the trail rejoins trail #18, turn right (south). Continue to the junction with trail #19, and turn right (west). This will return to your starting point.

For a longer hike, you can begin at the Elk Meadow trailhead. Begin east on trail #18 (Elk Meadow), and then follow the same route as above.

OUTLOOK RIDGE: Follow the main road through the park, just past the visitors' center, to the Outlook Ridge picnic area and trailhead. You will find water and a restroom at this trailhead. Trail #7 (Outlook Ridge) begins to the west from the picnic area. After 0.5 mile, you will pass three side trails: #8, 9, and 10, which all lead to overlook points. Each is a 0.5 mile out-and-back, and affords good views of the park.

Trail #7 ends at the junction with Trail #25 (Geer Pond); turn left (west). After 0.25 mile, pass Geer pond on your left (note that this part of the trail can be muddy). Bear right (north) onto Trail #26 (Beaver Ponds), continue to the junction with Trail #12 (Homestead), and turn right. As you near the Homestead trailhead, you will find Trail #1 (Revenuer's Ridge) to your right. This goes through the Lost Pond picnic area, then rejoins Trail #7. Turn left and return to the starting point.

Many other hikes are possible from here; Mueller is worth returning to over and over again—consult the trail map, available from the visitor's center, for details.

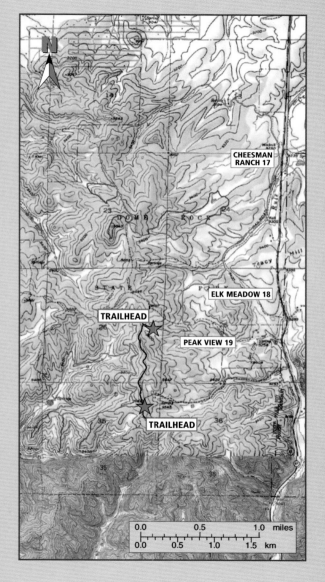

N

CHEESMAN
RANCH 17

ELK MEADOW 18

TRAILHEAD

PEAK VIEW 19

TRAILHEAD

| 0.0 | 0.5 | 1.0 miles |
| 0.0 | 0.5 | 1.0 | 1.5 km |

MUELLER STATE PARK

10. Palmer Lake Reservoirs and Cap Rock

BY BOB HOSTETLER

MAPS	Trails Illustrated, Pikes Peak/Cañon City, Number 137 USGS, Mt. Deception, 7.5 minute
ELEVATION GAIN	To second reservoir: 600 feet; to top of loop: 840 feet; to Cap Rock: 1,330 feet
RATING	Easy to scrambling/difficult
ROUND-TRIP DISTANCE	To second reservoir: 2.4 miles; for Ice Cave loop: 3.7 miles; for Cap Rock: 5.0 miles
ROUND-TRIP TIME	1–5 hours
NEAREST LANDMARK	Palmer Lake Town Hall

COMMENT: The two Palmer Lake Reservoirs and the area trails have a rich history dating to the last decades of the nineteenth century. The road to the reservoirs—built in 1887 and 1903—is occasionally used by maintenance vehicles and provides a steep, invigorating start to area hikes. Visiting the reservoirs alone provides excellent views in a peaceful valley and water setting. Heading out on one of the unimproved trails can feel like being in a very remote spot only a mile from the trailhead. Hikers who enjoy scrambling can reach a spectacular summit, the size of a dining room table, 250 feet above the ground on three sides. The early history of hiking in the area includes the second official hike by the CMC. This was on June 20, 1912, when Lucretia Vaile, an early Palmer Lake resident, led a group up the Reservoir Road, Balanced Rock Road, and Rampart Range Road to Woodland Park.

GETTING THERE: Take Interstate 25 to the Monument/Palmer Lake exit #161. Turn left onto Colorado 105 and follow it when it turns right after crossing I-25. Follow 105 for 3.8

Lower reservoir.

miles and watch for a Speed Limit 30 sign on the right and turn left onto South Valley Road (the road sign is not visible until after you've made the turn). Drive west on South Valley Road 0.4 mile and turn left on Old Carriage Road. Park at the bottom of the hill.

THE ROUTES:

PALMER LAKE RESERVOIRS: Hike west on the trail for 200 yards, until it joins the reservoir access road (FS322). Hike up this steep road for 0.6 mile to the first reservoir. Continue for 0.6 mile more to the second and much larger reservoir, a great spot for picnicking or fishing.

RESERVOIR/ICE CAVE CREEK LOOP: Follow the above route to the lower reservoir. At the upper end of the lower reservoir, the road takes a hard left and turns uphill. At this point (yellow trail on map), turn right, onto a rough, unimproved trail along the left side of Ice Cave Creek and its boulder field. (Ice Cave Creek is so-named because "caves" formed under the huge rocks in this canyon hold ice well into the summer. Be very careful attempting to explore these caves.) At 1.2 miles from the trailhead, cross the creek. At 1.4 miles, you will "T" into a north/south trail that shows evidence of having been a

Upper reservoir.

PHOTO BY BOB HOSTETLER

two track, four-wheel-drive road in years past. Turn south and follow this trail for 1.0 mile, back across Ice Cave Creek, up and over a ridge, then steeply down to an arm of the second reservoir, at 2.4 miles. Turn left to return to the trailhead.

CAP ROCK (a.k.a. ROCK DOME): An attempt on this rocky peak should be undertaken only by those comfortable with scrambling and some exposure. No technical climbing skills are required, however. This is the writer's favorite hike in the Monument/Palmer Lake area.

Follow the Reservoir/Ice Cave Creek route to the T intersection at 1.4 miles. Continue another 0.1 mile west to a meadow. Before crossing Ice Cave Creek again and going uphill, leave the trail and cross the meadow to a faint trail heading west-northwest that parallels Ice Cave Creek, going up and down the slope but averaging about 50 feet above the creek. Take in the view of Cap Rock—at this point the east and south walls will make it look like an unclimbable pillar. Just beyond the third little gully coming in from the right, angle up toward the southeast corner of the base of Cap Rock. Angle in to the rocks, toward a big tree, then angle right to stay under three house-sized rocks. Work through the rocks, staying 50–75 feet to the right of the east face of Cap Rock. When the terrain begins to flatten out, look left for a scramble up to the ramp that leads to the top. Enjoy the views and the big drops down the south and east faces. Return via the same route.

11. Pancake Rocks and Horsethief Park

BY BILL BROWN

MAPS	Trails Illustrated – Pikes Peak, Cañon City – Number 137
ELEVATION GAIN	1,400 feet
RATING	Moderate
ROUND-TRIP DISTANCE	6.25 miles
ROUND-TRIP TIME	4 hours
NEAREST LANDMARK	Divide

COMMENT: Horsethief Park and Pancake Rocks are popular four-season destinations. Families with children and others looking for a short hike will enjoy the 3.0 mile round trip to Horsethief Falls. It's a cool escape from summertime heat in the city. The longer trail to Pancake Rocks rewards hikers with unnatural looking stacks of saucer-shaped granite. It's hard to resist getting up close and personal to touch and climb onto some of these bizarre "pancakes".

In fall hunting season, hunters in blaze orange may be seen in Horsethief Park, reminding hikers to make themselves visible. By winter, snowshoers and backcountry skiers enjoy the area's high elevation, ample snowfall, and shaded north-facing slopes. Snow cover is usually reliable on forested slopes from late December to early April.

This entire hike is within the subalpine life zone. Blue spruce, limber pine, and aspen predominate, with some bristlecone pine at the higher elevations. The Ring the Peak Trail system, which is 80 percent complete, coincides with the Pancake Rocks Trail for about 2 miles.

GETTING THERE: From Colorado Springs, drive west on U.S. 24. Follow this highway 25 miles through Woodland Park to Divide. At the traffic light in Divide, turn left (south) on

Starting up the trail.

Colorado 67. At 9.1 miles, on the far side of a road cut that bypasses an abandoned railroad tunnel, there is a paved parking lot on the left with room for 10–15 cars. This is the trailhead.

THE ROUTE: The trail begins on the east side of the parking lot, just south of an interpretive sign about the history of the tunnel. After 100 yards, the trail makes a switchback to the left, and, in another 150 yards, it turns right. From here, it's a steady climb eastward on an old wagon road. After 0.5 mile on this road, the trail levels out, just past a short rocky section. Hundred-year-old barbed wire fences can be seen on each side of the trail at this point, a hint of the shady history of Horsethief Park, which you are now entering. After another 0.1 mile, you intersect the Ring the Peak (RTP) Trail. To the left would take you clockwise on the ring through Putney Gulch to the Crags area. Straight ahead (east) is the way to Pancake Rocks. Another 0.25 mile ahead is a sign marking another junction. Horsethief Falls is a worthwhile destination, 0.4 mile ahead.

A great spot for a pancake breakfast.   PHOTO BY PHOTO BY BILL BROWN

A right turn at the sign leads to Pancake Rocks. The next mile gains 800 feet of elevation, made easier by a series of well-constructed switchbacks. When the trail tops out, there's a view of a craggy high point just off the trail to the west, and distant views to the southwest. Continue on the trail, contouring generally southward, with a few minor ups and downs, for almost another mile. Cross a minor saddle; Pancake Rocks is another 600 yards to the south, through a grove of young aspen. Just before arriving, the Ring the Peak Trail diverges to the left, where it dead-ends, temporarily, pending access approvals and trail construction between here and the south slope of Pikes Peak.

At Pancake Rocks the view opens up toward Cripple Creek and the Sangre de Cristo Mountains to the southwest. Spectacular alpine expanses of the Pikes Peak Massif draw your eyes to the east. At your feet are slabs of Pikes Peak granite, with smaller piles of rock eroded into the pancake shapes that give this special place its name.

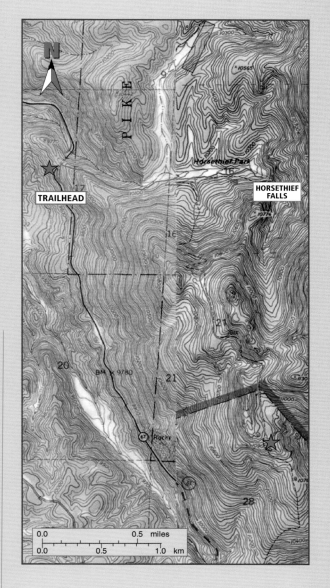

12. Pikes Peak from the Crags

BY MATT PIERCE

MAPS	Trails Illustrated, Pikes Peak/Cañon City, Number 137
ELEVATION GAIN	4,150 feet
RATING	Difficult
ROUND-TRIP DISTANCE	12.1 Miles
ROUND-TRIP TIME	7–10 Hours
NEAREST LANDMARK	Mueller State Park

COMMENT: Internationally known Pikes Peak, at 14,115 feet, towers over Colorado Springs and the Front Range. Hiking Pikes Peak is a challenging endeavor. While a 12.1 mile round trip in length, the Crags trailhead route is a preferable hike for many to the popular Barr Trail route, which is over 25 miles long and includes 7,000+ feet of elevation gain. The weather on Pikes Peak can be unpredictable at all times of the year. Be prepared and get an early start for this full day outing, especially in summer.

GETTING THERE: From Colorado Springs take U.S. 24 west. At the town of Divide, turn south (left) on Colorado 67 and drive 4.3 miles. Pass the entrance for Mueller State Park, on the right, and watch for Forest Service Road 383, on the left. Turn onto this dirt road and proceed 1.6 miles to the Rocky Mountain Mennonite Camp. Turn right and continue to the entrance to the campground, at mile 3.2. Drive through the campground to the loop at the end of the road.

In the future, the Forest Service plans to move the trailhead 0.25 mile down F.S. Road 383 from the Crags Campground, where there will be parking for 77 cars and a new restroom. The new trail will route you north of the campground and add approximately 1.2 miles round-trip to your hike. (See proposed trail in blue on map on page 101.)

The trail above the road.

PHOTO BY MATT PIERCE

THE ROUTE: Start hiking along the Crags Trail near the parking loop. Hike a few hundred yards before reaching a trail junction. Staying left will take you on Trail #664 towards the Crags. Stay right and cross over Fourmile Creek at a small footbridge. Start gaining some elevation through the trees. Pass a sign indicating you are headed towards The Devils Playground. At 1.7 miles, near 11,250 feet, the trail turns to the right. The next 1.0 mile after making this turn is some of the steepest and most difficult of this route, gaining 1,500 feet of elevation en route to the Devil's Playground, at 12,750 feet. Hike steadily up, leaving treeline, and reach the top of the slopes at 2.75 miles near 12,750 feet. From here, the hiking is easy for the next .75 mile as you hike through the Devils Playground. While passing, note a small summit just to the north. This is "The Devils Playground Peak" and is Teller County's Highpoint, at 13,070 feet. Visit this summit for some easy extra credit along your route.

Cross the Pikes Peak Highway at 3.5 miles (now near 13,000 feet,) where the trail continues along the east side of

The final push to the top.

the road. Continue hiking on the obvious trail, losing a little elevation as you parallel the road down to where it makes a right hand curve. Tempting as it may be, hiking is NOT permitted on the Pikes Peak Highway. With the exception of crossing the road near The Devils Playground, never hike directly on the road.

Near 4.25 miles, the trail can be difficult to follow, but the route in front of you is obvious. Leave the proximity of the road and begin hiking in a more direct line toward the southeast. Pass just to the left (east) of Point 13,363, before reaching the road again, near mile 5 and 13,200 feet. Pikes Peak is to the southeast, now just 1.1 miles and 900 feet of elevation away. Hike close to the road again for 0.2 mile before the road will make a turn off to the right (southwest). Continue away from the road on the obvious path to the base of the peak. The trail can be hard to follow in the last few hundred feet to the summit but it is marked with cairns that make navigation easier. Top out at the end of a large parking area. Hike through the parking lot to the summit house and the large sign marking the summit.

TRAILHEAD

13. Red Rock Canyon Open Space

BY GREG LONG

MAP	Trails Illustrated, Pikes Peak/Cañon City, Number 137
ELEVATION GAIN	400 feet
RATING	Easy
ROUND-TRIP DISTANCE	2.75 miles; 3 including Quarry option
ROUND-TRIP TIME	1–2 hours
NEAREST LANDMARK	U.S. 24 and 31st street.

COMMENT: At different times, Red Rock Canyon has been a stone quarry, a homestead, and a landfill. The City of Colorado Springs purchased the 785-acre property in 2003, making it one of the newest gems in the city park system. Its proximity makes it an ideal destination for an after-work jaunt or half-day outing. Red Rock Canyon has become popular with hikers, mountain bikers, equestrians, and rock climbers. With wide-open views and sandstone formations rivaling those in the Garden of the Gods, its popularity is no wonder.

Colorado Springs parks are open from dawn to dusk. Rock scrambling, defined as climbing more than 10 feet off the ground without safety equipment, is prohibited. Red Rock Canyon has porta-potties in its two parking lots and a small picnic area; there are no other facilities in the park.

GETTING THERE: Take U.S. 24 to the stoplight at 31st Street. Continue 0.4 mile past this light and look for a left turn lane. You will see a sign indicating High Street on your left and Ridge Road on your right. Take the left turn and then the next left into the park. Park in the first parking lot.

THE ROUTE: Red Rock Canyon has a varied collection of interconnecting trails; this description samples several of

Meadow near Homestead.

them with hopes you will be inspired to come back and sample more. The trails are well marked for easy navigation.

Walk from the west side of the parking lot onto a dirt road, then turn left at the trail sign onto the Sand Canyon Trail. At 0.3 mile, bear right (west) onto the Contemplative Trail. This trail is for hikers only, and many consider it the prettiest in the park. It passes beneath and between sandstone formations and features excellent views of Pikes Peak and the Pike National Forest, to the west, and the Garden of the Gods, to the north. Strategically placed benches allow for rest and quiet meditation.

Cross the Sand Canyon Trail at 0.9 miles and continue straight onto the Round Up Trail. The trail climbs steadily, crosses the Mesa Trail, at 1.4 miles, then reaches its high point at the junction with the Greenlee Trail, at 1.6 miles. Turn left (northeast) on the Greenlee Trail, which is actually an old road. The vegetation and rocks drop away and views of the park and surroundings are extensive as you wind back down into the canyon. Continue on the Greenlee Trail for

Passing through the quarry. PHOTO BY GREG LONG

about 1.0 mile, where it merges with the Mesa trail, to return to the parking lot.

For a slightly longer loop and a visit to a different part of the park, try this alternative: the Greenlee trail passes the Quarry Trail at 2.0 miles. Turn right to pass through a cut in the old quarry. Walk down steps carved in the stone. Descend from the quarry to the Red Rock Canyon Path, at 2.2 miles. Turn left (north) and follow this path to the site of the Bock family house. Transition to a dirt road and continue north past a picnic area to the upper parking lot. Follow a gravel path back to the lower lot.

SIDEBAR: CONNECT TO SECTION 16 TRAIL

Those seeking a bigger challenge should know that the trails of Red Rock Canyon connect with the Section 16 trail profiled on Hike 14 of this guide. String the two together into an all-day loop or set up a car shuttle at one of the trailheads. From the intersection of the Round Up and Greenlee trails described above, turn right and follow the Greenlee trail for 0.5 mile until it leaves the park, and follow the signs to its junction with the Section 16 Trail near the Intemann cutoff.

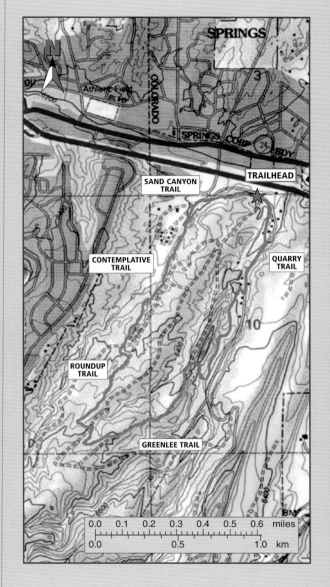

14. Section 16 – Palmer Red Rock Trail Loop

BY JESSICA MEHRING

MAPS	Trails Illustrated, Pikes Peak/Cañon City, Number 137
ELEVATION GAIN	1,200 feet
RATING	Moderate
ROUND-TRIP DISTANCE	5.6 miles
ROUND-TRIP TIME	2–4 hours
NEAREST LANDMARK	Red Rock Canyon

COMMENT: Section 16 and the Palmer Red Rock Trail provide a challenging and rewarding loop hike. You can go either clockwise or counterclockwise. Either way, the trail will incline during the first half and decline during the second—it has a pretty solid arc of elevation gain/loss, so not a lot of ups and downs. Counterclockwise is the easier route to follow and you get to enjoy the best mountain views during the longer downhill part of the trail. This direction is also more pleasant because you get the worst of the incline over more quickly, and the few mountain bikers that brave this trail usually go in the opposite direction, and you can see them coming. This hike is terrific year-round, but pack strap-on cleats in winter as the trail does get snow-covered and icy in spots. This hike provides gorgeous scenery, good photo ops, and plenty of challenge without having to go too far from the city.

GETTING THERE: From Interstate 25, take the U.S. 24/Cimarron exit west. Continue west for 2 miles and turn left on 26th Street. Drive 1.4 miles to the four-way stop sign. Turn right at the stop sign onto Gold Camp Road. Continue for 0.8 mile, to a small parking lot on the right. A large sign saying *Section 16* is in the middle of this lot: this is the trailhead. If the lot is full, there is more parking ahead, on the left side of the road.

Starting out.

PHOTO BY JESSICA MEHRING

THE ROUTE: Start at the Section 16 trailhead. The first part of the
loop is Section 16, with a bright red dirt trail and interesting
rock formations. After the first 0.5 mile or so, the trail wraps
to the left with stunning views of the city to the right. A few
small trails will shoot off left and right, but stay on the well-
worn path.

At the Intemann Trailhead sign, continue straight to where
Section 16 becomes the Palmer Red Rock Trail. (To stay on
the correct trail, look for markers that say Palmer Red Rock
and Ring the Peak.) After this point, the incline becomes
more difficult, and you have a straight climb upward. The
trail soon enters the cool woods, though, and the greenery
and abundant wildlife make the climb a bit more pleasant. At
about the 1.7 mile mark, the worst of the climb is over and
the switchbacks begin. The crest of the incline is at 2.0 miles,
and it is all downhill from there. Breathtaking views make
the easy second part of the trail hurry by. At about the 2.8-
mile mark, a lovely little spring makes a perfect resting place
in the warmer months. At about the 4.5 mile mark, the trail

Gentle ups and downs on the trail.

splits—take the right fork. Shortly after the fork, you will come to a dirt road—High Drive. Turn left and follow High Drive. Be aware that a few cars might drive by in summer. (The road is closed to traffic in the winter, and is a perfect for snowshoeing after a good snowstorm). Bear Creek follows High Drive a good ways, with lots of places to stop off and enjoy the water in the summer. After a little less than a mile, High Drive meets up with paved roads and you come out at the junction of Gold Camp Road and Bear Creek Road. Walk left to get onto Gold Camp Road and continue less than 0.3 miles to get back to the Section 16 trailhead parking area.

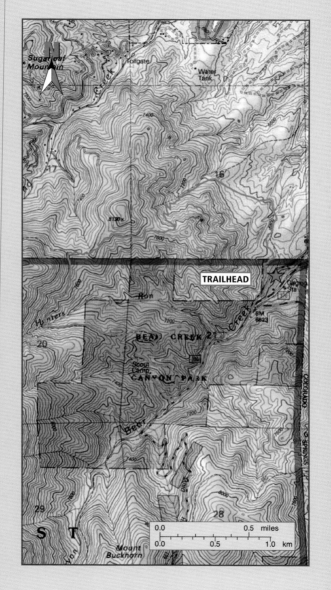

TRAILHEAD

15. Seven Bridges Trail to Jones Park to Mt. Buckhorn Trail Loop

BY ERIN SHAW

MAPS	Trails Illustrated, Pikes Peak/Cañon City, Number 137
ELEVATION GAIN	Loop: 2,000 feet; Seven Bridges: 1,000 feet
RATING	Loop: Moderate–difficult; Seven Bridges: easy–moderate
ROUND-TRIP DISTANCE	Loop: approx. 9.5 miles; Seven Bridges: approx. 3.5 miles
ROUND-TRIP TIME	Loop: 4–5 hours; Seven Bridges: 1.5 hours
NEAREST LANDMARK	Helen Hunt Falls

COMMENT: North Cheyenne Cañon is an understandably popular destination. The Pikes Peak granite creates a stunning, craggy invitation to delve deep into the canyon. Seven Bridges is a very popular trail in the park, and offers an ideal family outing, crossing North Cheyenne Creek seven times over rustic wooden footbridges. Wildflowers are plentiful and there are many nice lunch spots along the trail. Turn after the seventh bridge, or continue to Jones Park, a valley with aspen and coniferous trees, where the trail meets Bear Creek and offers views of nearby peaks, hidden waterfalls, wildflowers, and a variety of birds.

Bicycles are allowed along the entire loop, and motorized bikes may travel the trails around Jones Park and Mt. Buckhorn. It can be more peaceful to take the hike on a weekday.

GETTING THERE: From Interstate 25, take the Nevada Avenue/ Tejon Street exit 140 and proceed south 0.4 mile on South Tejon Street to the junction of Tejon, Ramona, and West

Bridge Three.

Cheyenne Boulevard. Veer right (southwest) onto West
Cheyenne Boulevard and drive 2.5 miles to the junction with
North Cheyenne Canyon Road. The Starsmore Discovery
Visitor Center is located at this junction. Turn right, entering
North Cheyenne Canyon Park, and continue up North Cheyenne
Canyon Road, past Helen Hunt Falls, for 3.2 miles to "the
hub" parking area at the junction of Gold Camp Road, High
Drive, and North Cheyenne Canyon Road.

THE ROUTE: Begin at the gate on the west end of the lot and
follow a dirt road for 0.75 mile. Pass one trail to your right
and look for a second trail, just beyond a sign that reads

Falls above Seventh Bridge.

North Cheyenne Creek. Turn right onto the trail and soon cross the first footbridge. Other trails intersect the main trail above here; stay on the trail that climbs up the canyon parallel with the creek. Over the next 1.0 mile, you will cross six more bridges. In the winter this portion of the trail is usually covered in ice and extra traction on hiking boots is recommended.

Continue to climb through the canyon to reach Jones Park. Look for the trail just beyond the last bridge that climbs up and to the right of the creek. Views of the creek below reveal a few small waterfalls.

Signage is sparse. Social trails diverge from the main trail, but they meet it again. After rising above the creek for 0.5 mile, the trail and the creek meet again. The Pipeline Trail comes in from the left (southwest) shortly after this junction; be sure to stay on the Seven Bridges Trail, heading west-northwest.

As the trail enters a mixed forest, turn left at an unmarked intersection. The trail soon meets up with the Pipeline Trail again; stay straight and don't cross the creek. Over the next 1.0 mile, stay straight on the main trail and cross two streams before coming to another unmarked intersection. Turn right and head east-southeast. Stay on the main trail as it turns right and crosses another stream. After 0.2 mile there is a large open area where trails merge. To complete the loop, turn left onto the marked Bear Creek Trail.

View of Colorado Springs.

Columbine.

PHOTO BY ERIN SHAW

Follow Bear Creek for about 1.3 miles to a trail junction; leave Bear Creek trail and cross the creek to the right. Immediately begin climbing a steep ridge. After about 0.4 mile, the trail follows another ridge, rising to the right. The ridge top affords spectacular views of Colorado Springs and Cheyenne Mountain.

For the next 1.0 mile, the trail continues to follow the north side of this ridge before meeting another ridge, which the trail now follows from the south. Shortly after leaving this ridge, an unmarked trail comes in from the right. This is the Buckhorn Cutoff Trail; follow it for approximately 1.2 miles, avoiding social trails, to rejoin the Seven Bridges Trail above the first bridge. Turn left to return to the dirt road and parking lot.

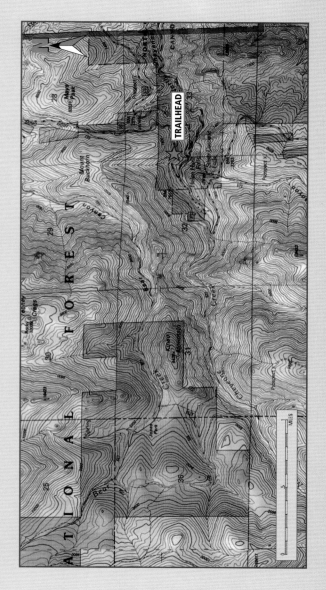

TRAILHEAD

16. St. Mary's Falls Trail and Mount Rosa

BY DAN ANDERSON

MAPS	Trails Illustrated, Pikes Peak/Cañon City, Number 137 (Cuts off Mount Rosa) USGS, Manitou Springs, 7.5 minute Pikes Peak Atlas
ELEVATION GAIN	St. Mary's Falls base: 1,500 feet Mount Rosa: 4,100 feet
RATING	St. Mary's Falls base: easy–moderate Mount Rosa: moderate–difficult
ROUND-TRIP DISTANCE	St. Mary's Falls base: 6 miles Mount Rosa: 13.8 miles
ROUND-TRIP TIME	St. Mary's Falls base: 2.5–4 hours Mount Rosa: 7–10 hours
NEAREST LANDMARK	Colorado Springs, North Cheyenne Cañon Park

COMMENT: This is a great hike up a lovely side canyon of North Cheyenne Canyon. An inviting place on a hot day, the trail follows along a stream to a waterfall. It is enjoyed best in late spring and early summer when more water comes tumbling down. It can be either a hike or a snowshoe outing after a good snowfall, but be careful of ice near the falls.

GETTING THERE: From Interstate 25, take the Nevada Avenue/ Tejon Street exit 140 and proceed south 0.4 mile on South Tejon Street to the junction of Tejon, Ramona, and West Cheyenne Boulevard. Veer right (southwest) onto West Cheyenne Boulevard and drive 2.5 miles to the junction with North Cheyenne Canyon Road. The Starsmore Discovery Visitor Center is located at this junction. Turn right, entering North Cheyenne Canyon Park, and continue up North Cheyenne Canyon Road, past Helen Hunt Falls, for 3.2 miles to "the hub" parking area at the junction of Gold Camp Road, High Drive, and North Cheyenne Canyon Road.

Topping out Mount Rosa.

PHOTO BY DAN ANDERSON

THE ROUTES:

ST. MARY'S FALLS TRAIL NUMBER 624: This hike starts at a parking area known as "the hub." It follows Gold Camp Road, which leaves past the gate at the west end of the parking lot and is currently closed to cars. The road makes a long horseshoe and reaches collapsed tunnel number 3. Take the trail to the left of the tunnel up and over to a trail junction. The St. Mary's Falls Trail is the right fork. The left fork goes down to Gold Camp Road, on the other side of the tunnel.

The St. Mary's Falls Trail heads south up Buffalo Canyon. The trail gains elevation slowly at first, then becomes steeper near the falls. There are a couple of switchbacks to get to the base of the falls. The trail to the falls is a 1.0 mile side trip from the second leg of the switchbacks. If you wish to continue on, eight more switchbacks will take you up the hillside. The last switchback is a long leg back to the vicinity of the creek. There is a primitive trail down to the top of the falls from here. Be careful if you go down there—the steep hillside is very treacherous near the falls.

Pikes Peak from Mount Rosa.

PHOTO BY DAN ANDERSON

MOUNT ROSA, NELSONS TRAIL NUMBER 672: From the top of St. Mary's Falls, the trail continues up the canyon until it reaches an old road. At this point, the standard route continues up the old road to the junction of Forest Service Road 381. This is the official end of the St. Mary's Falls Trail. Turn right (north) and go about 220 feet to the junction of Nelsons Trail on the left (west) side of the road. This trail climbs steadily, with many switchbacks, to a large shoulder on the north side of Mount Rosa. Head south along the flat to a trail junction (Trail 673) just before the terrain turns uphill. The trail curving to the right (west) goes down to Frostys Park. Continue on the trail straight ahead, which is easy to miss, as it climbs the north ridge to the top of Mount Rosa.

On your way up Mount Rosa, there's a second, smaller shoulder. This is a great place for pictures of Pikes Peak and Almagre Mountain before reaching the summit.

After hiking up the last 500 feet, you will be treated to a grand view. Zebulon Pike called the tall peak in the distance Grand Peak; we now call it Pikes Peak. Research by John Murphy has determined that Pike probably reached Mount Rosa and turned back, declaring that Grand Peak would never be climbed.

SIDEBAR: A SIDE TRIP

Above St. Mary's Falls, where the single-track trail turns into the old road, a primitive trail branches to the left and continues up the canyon, closer to the stream. For those with good route-finding skills, this side trip is my favorite way up the canyon. If you stay with this trail, it ends 1.2 miles later at an old quarry where it meets Forest Service Road 381. Turn right and go north for 0.55 miles to the junction of the Nelsons Trail.

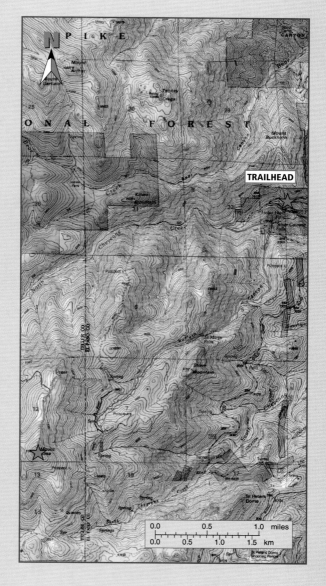

17. Stanley Canyon Trail

BY UWE K. SARTORI

MAPS	Trails Illustrated – Pikes Peak/Cañon City, Number 137 USGS, Cascade, 7.5 minute
ELEVATION GAIN	1,450 feet
RATING	Moderate
ROUND-TRIP DISTANCE	3.8 miles
ROUND-TRIP TIME	2–3 hours
NEAREST LANDMARK	Air Force Academy Hospital

COMMENT: The U.S. Air Force Academy is a major landmark in the Colorado Springs area. Located on 18,000 pristine acres, the Academy is home to the popular Stanley Canyon Trail and offers a wonderful three-season sample of the Pikes Peak area's eastern slope.

Enjoy a gentle hike beside a stream under an aspen canopy that leads into a meadow carpeted with alpine flowers, as well as steep hiking that gets the heart pumping. Challenge yourself by scrambling up granite rock. Soak in gorgeous vistas of the Academy, the Black Forest area, and northern Colorado Springs—including towering granite outcroppings, alpine forests, and waterfalls. Count on varied flora and local wildlife to add color and excitement to your hiking experience.

The reward for your effort is the beautiful Stanley Reservoir. Here, you can relax and enjoy your time on the shoreline (no swimming allowed) before heading back down. Make this a day outing with a family picnic at the reservoir. Afterwards, enjoy a tour of the Academy grounds.

For the best experience, hike this trail between late May and early October. Late fall, winter, and early spring seasons bring winter conditions that make this trail potentially dangerous. This hike is not suitable for strollers or walkers. Mountain

Entering the meadow near the top.

bikes are not recommended. The trail contains some steep, strenuous sections and requires a little scrambling.

GETTING THERE: From Interstate 25, take exit 156B-N. Entrance/Air Force Academy. Be prepared to stop at the gate and show your ID. Drive 0.5 mile and go left onto Stadium Blvd. Go 1.2 miles and turn right, onto Academy Drive. Drive 2.4 miles and turn left, onto Pine Drive. Go 0.2 mile and turn right, onto an unmarked dirt road (just past the AFA hospital). Drive 0.6 mile to the trailhead. From the south entrance of the Academy, drive north on South Gate Boulevard to Pine Drive. Turn left onto Pine Drive and travel 3.9 miles to the unmarked dirt road on the left. From this direction, you will almost certainly drive past the road; turn around when you get to the hospital.

THE ROUTE: Walk past the gate at the trailhead to the road. Shortly after starting up the road, take a left fork. Less than 75 yards after the fork, a sign directs you to the right. Walk

Stanley Reservoir.

PHOTO BY UWE K. SARTORI

another 100 yards and turn left at the next sign for Stanley Reservoir 707.

Be ready for a mile of steep, loose dirt and gravel on the trail. While ascending, first listen, and then look, for a small waterfall to the left. Further up, the trail will appear to overlap with a stream. Continue on, staying close and to the right of the stream. Resist the temptation to angle steeply up to the right as it leads off trail. There are some sections that give the opportunity to do a little scrambling on the granite rock. One short section involves hopping over rocks in the stream itself. Be careful: wet rock and wet boots make for a slippery climb.

After the first mile, the trail mellows into a gentle hike. Pass through a small meadow and into a tree-canopied section over a stream crossing, complete with a makeshift log bridge. Soon, cross the stream again. For the last 0.5 mile, enjoy the trail as it alternates between meadows and trees, finally winding its way through a large meadow to the bottom of the reservoir dam. From here, a short trail to the left brings you to the shore of the reservoir.

SIDEBAR: **AIR FORCE ACADEMY**

The Air Force Academy visitor hours are from 8:00 a.m. to 6:00 p.m. Some of the trail is on Air Force Academy property, which means you are subject to their jurisdiction. The remainder of the trail and the reservoir is in the Pike National Forest.

18. Talon Trail

BY CAROL NUGENT

MAPS	Trails Illustrated, Pikes Peak/Cañon City, Number 137
	Cheyenne Mountain State Park Trail Map http://parks.state.co.us/Parks/cheyennemountain
ELEVATION GAIN	993 feet
RATING	Easy
ROUND-TRIP DISTANCE	5.25 miles
ROUND-TRIP TIME	2–3 hours
NEAREST LANDMARK	Cheyenne Mountain State Park

COMMENT: The Talon Trail in Cheyenne Mountain State Park will lead the almost-urban hiker from rolling grasslands to ponderosa forests. The first third of the trail takes you through grassy foothills, with prairie dog homes on the east side of the trail and rabbits and deer often visible to the west. As you continue up the trail, the grassland is soon mixed with groves of gambel oak. Hummingbirds may zoom past and land on a nearby limb, showing off their fancy emerald green markings. Soon enough, you climb into the ponderosa forests, where woodpeckers knock about with mechanical regularity.

The trail is at least three feet wide its entire length, covered with pea-sized gravel, and graded for easy walking. The trail is multi-use and your author has encountered a five-year-old mountain biker touring with his family. By the end of the trail, you will have been treated to spectacular views of the cliffs on Cheyenne Mountain.

At several points along the way, you will find trail maps. On each map, the trails are color-coded. Rather than the more common trail signs—with trail names, arrows, and mileage—colored markers designate the trails in the park. The color of the disk corresponds to the color of the trail on

Diverse ecozones.

PHOTO BY BILL BROWN

the trailside signs and on the trail map issued at the entrance. At each trail intersection, look for the trail markers located approximately 20 feet up each trail.

GETTING THERE: Take Interstate 25 to South Nevada (Exit 140). Turn south on Nevada Avenue. Nevada turns into Highway 115. Travel south for approximately 5.0 miles to the park entrance. Turn west and follow the road into the park. If you do not have a State Parks pass, there is an entrance fee per day per vehicle. When you pay the fee, you will receive a trail map. To park for the Talon Trail, go to the Day Use trailhead.

THE ROUTE: The Talon Trail is an out-and-back, 5.25 mile, trail that begins on the west side of the parking lot near the restrooms. As you leave the parking lot, follow the yellow markers. The Talon Trail intersects with the Zook Loop (marked with blue). Follow the Zook markers to the first trail to the left, marked with yellow. Stay on the trail marked with yellow until the end of the trail.

A well-groomed footpath.

For the return trip, you have the option of turning around and heading back to your vehicle, or you can add a little extra to your trip by taking either the South Talon Trail (orange markers) or North Talon Trail (green markers). For this trail description, the author opted for the North Talon Trail. That trail, listed as 1.6 miles, looks fearsome on the map, but the grade is never more than what you have already climbed. The trail takes you to the top of a ridge, with views of the cliffs on Cheyenne Mountain, a canyon dropping away below, and the not-very-distant city. Follow the North Talon green markers back to Talon, and then follow the yellow markers back to the trailhead.

SIDEBAR: **GEOCACHING**

GPS coordinates are provided all along the trail. The points are referenced in longitude and latitude. As part of the Park's GPS initiative, the park supports geocaching—sort of like treasure hunting—and rents out GPS units at the Visitor Center.

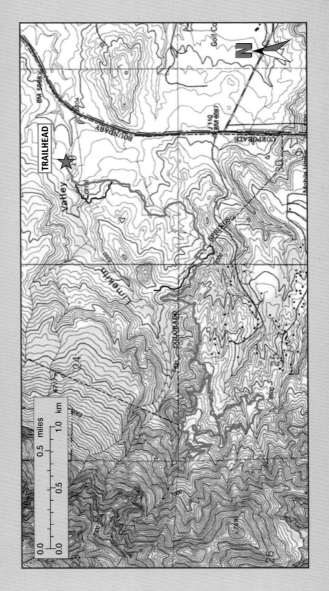

19. Templeton Trail – Palmer Park

BY BILL HOUGHTON

MAPS	USGS, Colorado Springs/Pikeview, 7.5 minute Sanborn Maps – Palmer Park
ELEVATION GAIN	Numerous ups and downs, but no sustained gain
RATING	Easy
ROUND-TRIP DISTANCE	3.8 miles
ROUND-TRIP TIME	3 hours
NEAREST LANDMARK	Colorado Springs

COMMENT: At 730 acres, Palmer Park was one of the larger parkland parcels given by Gen. William Jackson Palmer to the citizens of the city he founded: Colorado Springs. The Templeton Trail in Palmer Park is a trail for all seasons. Unlike its neighboring trails up slope or down, it has good shade for hot summer days. On the occasional cold, snowy day in winter there is a warm side that catches the sun but is sheltered from the wind. Much of the trail is rock, so the rains create only a few puddles of mud.

GETTING THERE: Situated near the geographic center of Colorado Springs, Palmer Park is loosely bounded by Austin Bluffs Parkway on the north, Academy Boulevard on the east, Maizeland Road on the south and Union Boulevard on the west. The main entrance is on Maizeland, 0.2 mile west of Academy. Turn north into the park and proceed 0.9 mile to a turnoff—a dirt road to the right. Follow it to the Yucca Flats parking area at the end of the road.

THE ROUTE: Templeton Trail is a loop that starts and ends at the parking area. Hiking toward the south and west takes you to the sunny side. Hiking north and eventually west offers the

Weathered rock.

shaded, cooler side. Based on the season, temperature and time of day, you can choose the best way to hike the trail.

We will describe the loop in a counter-clockwise direction, starting from the north mesa parking lot. Proceed north on the off-leash Mesa Trail. After about 100 yards, there is a signed trail off to the right. This is the Templeton Trail; follow it sharply downhill. As the trail levels out, you begin to get a feel for what much of the trail will be like: contouring along the upper slope of the mesa while passing over, under, around, and through rock formations made mostly of soft, coarse sandstone.

This eastern side of the loop allows some views, but is mostly forested as it winds its way north. At about 0.6 mile, there is a confusing hub of trails. The Templeton Trail is slightly to the left. A wider trail comes down from the mesa and descends to the Lazy Land picnic area, which in turn is a short stroll from curbside parking on Brenner Place, just off Austin Bluffs Parkway.

After a distinctive descent, and intersection with another opportunity to get to Lazy Land, an uphill section leads to the most impressive feature of the entire loop, the Sunrise Sentinel. This is an impressive hoodoo with a very large cap for his narrow neck, offering good views to the east. Please respect the fragility of this and other formations in this area. The Sunrise Sentinel comes just before the northeast corner, where the trail turns west at 1.1 miles.

This northern leg is obviously too short for its wonderful forested path. Walk a bit slower and enjoy it a little longer. About 100 yards before the northwest corner, a rough trail scrambles down the hill. Ignore this one and stick to the more obvious trail. At the corner (1.4 miles) is another impressive rock, more robust and colorful than the Sunrise Sentinel. Good views of the UCCS campus, the Garden of the Gods, and Pikes Peak make this a good place to sit and enjoy the day.

The Sunrise Sentinel.

A serious balancing act.

PHOTO BY BILL HOUGHTON

The southbound, western leg of the loop is an enjoyable, shaded route that consists more of scrub oak than conifer. It takes you just below several cliff faces. In one place the wind and water have hollowed out an overhang that almost qualifies as a cave. Short ups and downs make this leg a good workout. At the southwest corner, 2.0 miles, you have completed only about half of the loop. The distinctive cliffs and crumbling sandstone attest to the fragile nature of this environment.

Just past the corner, the trail becomes obscure. Look up and climb a bit of sandstone to find the trail. This southern leg contours in and out of a number of canyons carved in the mesa. After the first in-and-out, there is an opportunity to descend to another parking lot near the Reyner Stables, off Paseo Road, followed by a chance to leave the trail and go onto the mesa. Continue on—the best is yet to come.

Nature at her best.

The second in-and-out has a great platform with good views to the south and a chance to see where the trail is taking you. Continuing on this in-and-out leads to a favorite location: the valley of the druids, with an amazing druid-priest at the top. Be sure to spend some time here seeking the formations below the trail that include another hoodoo, a balanced rock, and great color. Behind the large druid-priest is a fantasy backdrop of carved sandstone.

Continue on through several more indentations until a distinct turn north brings you back to the Yucca Flats parking lot, at 3.8 miles.

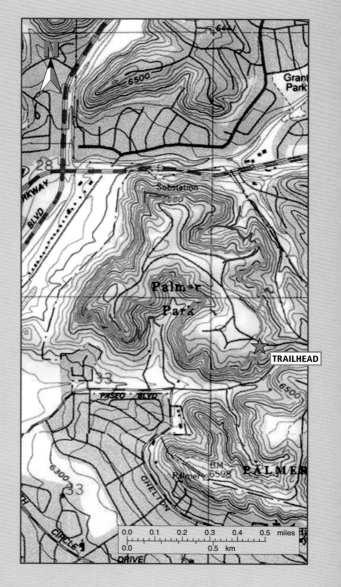

20. The Crags Trail

BY ERIC SWAB

MAPS	Trails Illustrated, Pikes Peak/Cañon City, Number 137 USGS, Woodland Park/Pikes Peak, 7.5 minute
ELEVATION GAIN	724 feet
RATING	Easy–moderate
ROUND-TRIP DISTANCE	4.3 miles (5.5 miles from proposed trailhead)
ROUND-TRIP TIME	3 hours
NEAREST LANDMARK	Mueller State Park

COMMENT: The Crags Trail is a prime example of a simple hike with a great reward. After hiking through the Four Mile Creek valley with its lush meadows, rocky spires, and aspen and pine forests, you end up atop a rocky outcrop with gnarled old limber pines and great views. The Crags is a four-season favorite with hikers, skiers, and snowshoers. It receives and holds snow longer than most other areas on Pikes Peak.

GETTING THERE: From Colorado Springs, take U.S. 24 west. At the town of Divide, turn south (left) on Colorado 67 and drive 4.3 miles. After you pass the entrance for Mueller State Park on your right, watch for Forest Service Road 383 on your left. Turn onto this dirt road and proceed 1.6 miles to the Rocky Mountain Mennonite Camp. Turn right and continue to the entrance to the campground, at 3.2 miles. Drive through the campground to the loop at the end of the road. The trailhead and a restroom are at the far end of the Crags Campground Road. There is no fee for parking at the trailhead.

In winter the road is generally plowed to the parking area just past the Mennonite Camp, so you may have to ski or snowshoe farther than indicated on the map.

Along the Crags Trail.

In the future, the Forest Service plans to move the trailhead 0.25 mile down F.S. Road 383 from the Crags Campground, with a new restroom and parking for up to 77 cars. The new trail would pass north of the campground and add aproximately 1.2 miles round-trip to your hike. (See the proposed trail in blue on the map.)

ROUTE: A well-marked and well-traveled trail starts at the east end of the parking loop. At 0.2 mile, come to the junction of Forest Trails 664 and 753 (old 664A). Stay left on 664. (Trail 753 goes to the summit of Pikes Peak, a hike that is described on page 62.)

At 1.0 mile, come to a sometimes-marshy area at the mouth of a side canyon. Cross the drainage and stay to the right of the magnificent pile of rocks ahead of you. The valley begins to narrow at 1.5 miles. On your right you will see a shallow cave near the bottom of another pile of rock. A little farther on, another trail splits off to the left; stay straight here. At 1.7 miles, begin the final climb of 300 feet to the high

Rock formations abound on the trail.

point of the Crags. Watch your footing—the decomposed granite can be very slippery.

We recommend that you return by the same route. However, if you are a good route finder you may pick up another faint trail by turning left at the rock with the cave. This is sometimes called the "Shady Side Trail" and is popular with skiers and snowshoers because it holds the snow longer. This route parallels Trail 664, but stays on the opposite side of the valley and joins Trail 753 at a sign that says *Devils Playground left, and Crags C.G., to the right.* Go to the right and you will cross the creek and arrive at the intersection of Trails 664 and 753.

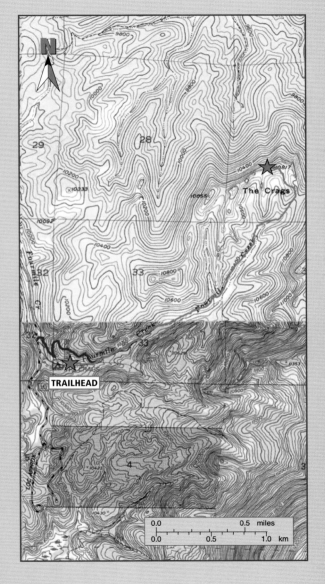

TRAILHEAD

The Crags

0.0 0.5 miles
0.0 0.5 1.0 km

Colorado Weather

Somewhere in the state of Colorado, it snows every single day of the year. Somewhere in the state of Colorado, someone is wearing shorts every single day of the year. Welcome to the strange and variable world of Colorado weather. Predictable only in its unpredictability, the weather in the mountains and along the Front Range demands constant vigilance and a really good layering system.

At its most basic level, however, dealing with the weather in Colorado can boiled down to two words: *leave early.* Despite the seeming chaos of our weather patterns, visitors and new residents often notice a certain predictability about our summertime forecasts: chances are, the local TV weatherperson will be calling for sunny with a chance of thunderstorms in the afternoon. Whether climbing in the foothills or the high country, starting your hike early and planning to be heading down by midday adds a measure of safety to your trip. This is particularly crucial if your plans will take you above treeline—a climb up Pikes Peak, for example. Afternoon thunderstorms move in fast and catch many hikers unaware. If you see a storm building, prudence suggests a hasty retreat. Colorado is number two in the nation in lightning deaths—don't add to those statistics.

While summer has its lightning storms, spring and fall can bring sudden, radical, temperature shifts and the need to be in shorts one minute and huddled against a blizzard the next. Always be prepared with extra layers, just in case. Winter brings with it sunshine and cold, clear days, along with blizzards that can last for days.

Colorado is home to many excellent volunteer search and rescue teams. Bringing the proper gear and paying attention to the weather can prevent your getting to know one of these teams.

About the Author

Greg Long began hiking with the Boy Scouts at age eleven and hasn't stopped since. His outdoor adventures have taken him all over the United States and the world. Among his accomplishments, he is particularly proud of a thru-hike of the Appalachian Trail in 1990, a climb to the central summit of Shisha Pangma in Tibet (8,013 meters/26,300 feet) in 2005, and a solo ascent of Pequeño Alpamayo in Bolivia (5,460 meters/17,900 feet) in 2006. Greg's favorite times, however, are when he is exploring the many trails of the Pike National Forest near his home in Palmer Lake. A couple of those trails appear in this guide; many do not (and he's not telling).

Greg funds his outdoor adventures by teaching language arts, social studies, and physical education in the Options 38 program at Lewis–Palmer High School in Monument.

A trail of sandstone leads north, Red Rock Canyon Open Space.

PHOTO BY GREG LONG

Checklist

The Best Colorado Springs Hikes